ESSENTIAL
FASHION
ILLUSTRATION
POSES

D1295143

ROCKPORT

ESSENTIAL
FASHION
ILLUSTRATION
POSES

GLOUCESTER MASSACHUSETTS

ROCKPORT
PUBLISHERS

Copyright © 2007 by maomao publications
First published in 2007 in the United States of America by
Rockport Publishers, a member of
Quayside Publishing Group
33 Commercial Street
Gloucester, MA 01930-0589
Telephone: (978) 282-9590
Fax: (978) 283-2742
www.rockpub.com

ISBN-13: 978-1-59253-330-5
ISBN-10: 1-59253-330-2

10 9 8 7 6 5 4 3 2 1

Publisher: Paco Asensio

Editorial coordination: Catherine Collin

Art director: Mireia Casanovas Soley

Graphic design and layout: Anabel Naranjo

Illustrations: Maite Lafuente, Javier Navarro, Juanjo Navarro

Introduction: Ana G. Cañizares

Editorial project:
maomao publications
C/ Tallers 22 bis, 3° 1ª
08001 Barcelona. Spain
Tel.: +34 93 481 57 22
Fax: +34 93 317 42 08
www.maomaopublications.com

Printed in Spain

Contents

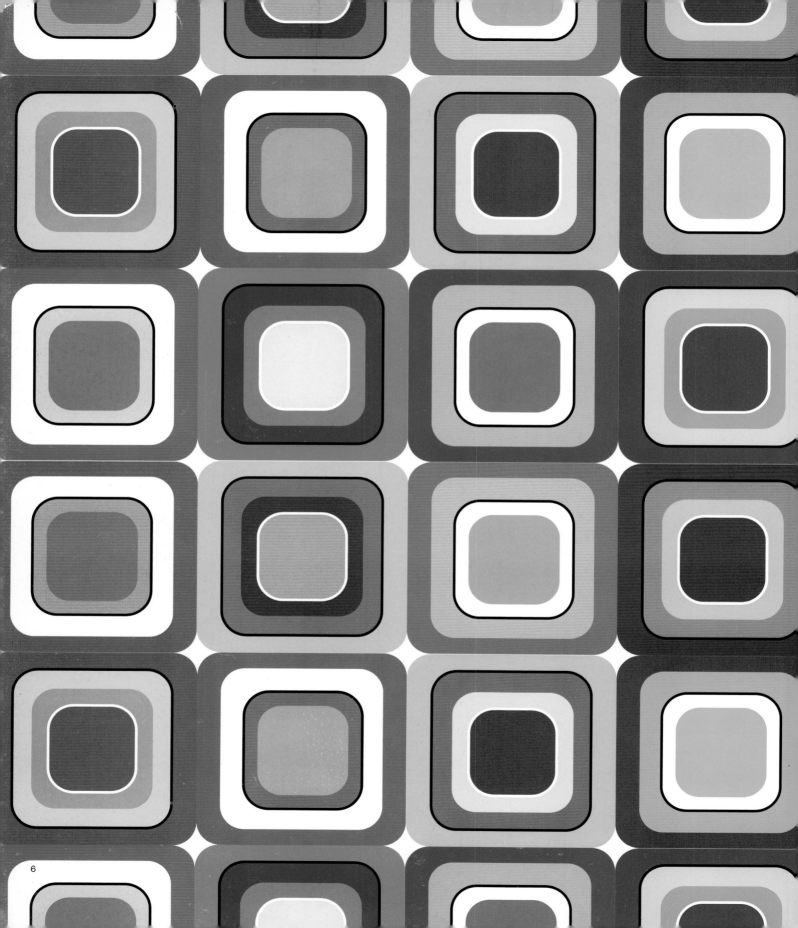

Introduction

As with all creative processes, the materialization of a particular design must begin as a concept and pass through several stages of realization. Perhaps the most important of these stages is the transferral of the initial idea onto paper in order to be able to turn that drawing into a real object. In the realm of fashion, the illustration of garments and accessories on human figures is crucial in transmitting their physical and stylistic qualities, exemplifying how a piece of clothing should look when worn and how the fabric falls in different poses. Capturing the essence of these designs, however, requires skill and an understanding of drawing techniques essential to fashion illustration. This book serves as a tool in perfecting these techniques to ensure an ideal representation of clothing designs in different poses.

Knowledge of anatomical proportions, expressing the appropriate shifts in weight in different poses and angles and producing the varying effects of different fabrics in a realistic and natural manner are some of the basic techniques explained within this compilation, which can be used as a foundation for developing a unique and personal style of illustration. Approximately 170 poses that are frequently used in the world of fashion illustration ranging from static, frontal views to turning, walking, dancing and sitting positions, are shown. Starting with semi-naked poses, the figures are dressed with three different categories of clothing, depicting the fall of diverse fabrics on the body.

The garments featured take on a myriad of shapes, textures and forms, including patterns, leather, knitwear, lightweight fabrics, heavy fabrics, transparent, sheen, compact, voluminous, and so on. These examples reflect the most popular and up-to-date design trends in the industry, and they will help you create your own drawings. A tool for aspiring fashion designers or those simply interested in learning new illustration techniques, this attractive and practical manual provides the necessary skills and offers a wealth of inspiration for perfecting the fascinating art of fashion illustration.

Ana G. Cañizares

Body and Proportions

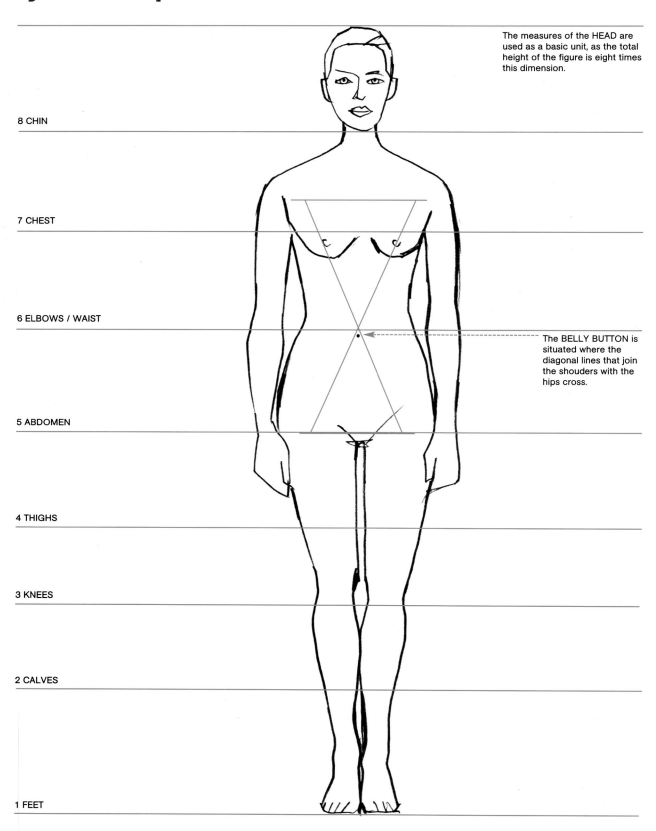

The measures of the HEAD are used as a basic unit, as the total height of the figure is eight times this dimension.

8 CHIN

7 CHEST

6 ELBOWS / WAIST

The BELLY BUTTON is situated where the diagonal lines that join the shoulders with the hips cross.

5 ABDOMEN

4 THIGHS

3 KNEES

2 CALVES

1 FEET

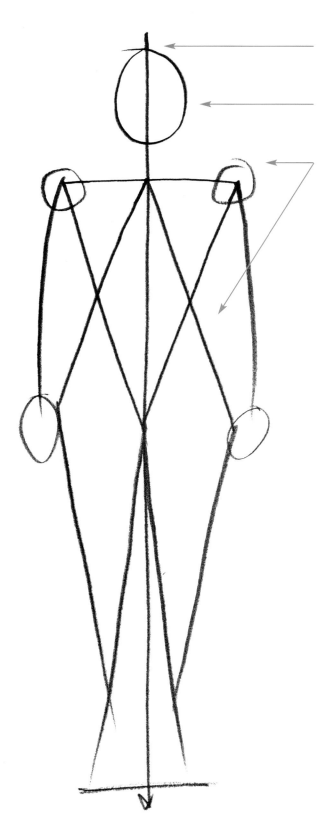

1. CENTRE OF BALANCE
   Achieved by drawing a vertical line that divides the body into two symmetrical halves.

2. HEAD
   A circle can be used as a base on which to define the size and inclination of the body.

3. SHOULDERS AND HIPS
   These four points must be perfectly balanced to correctly distribute the weight of the figure.

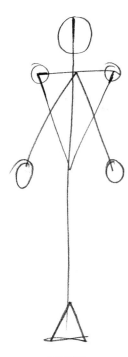

Standing

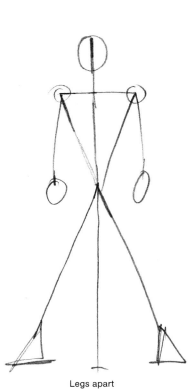

Legs apart

Walking

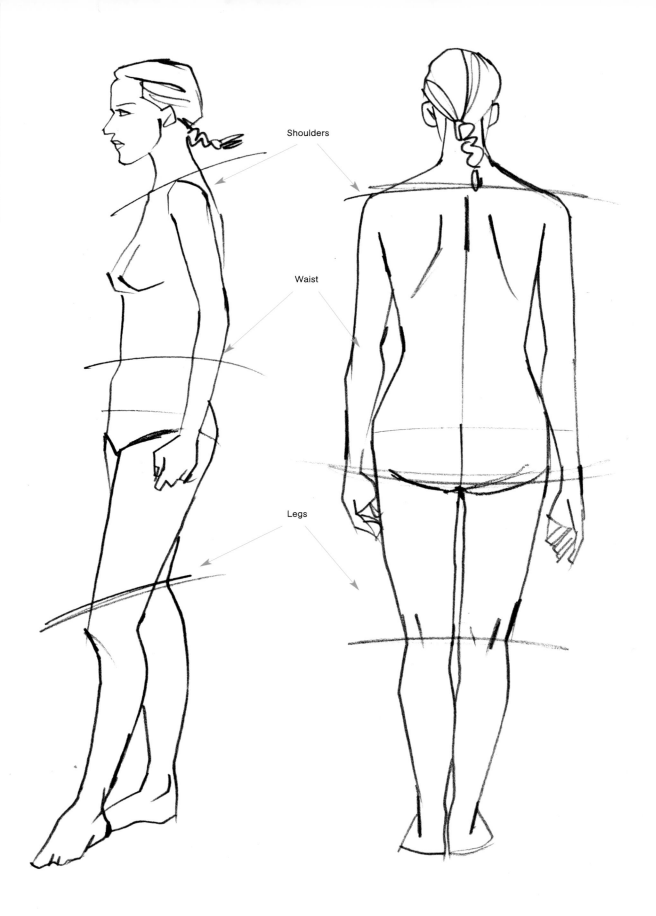

Shoulders

Waist

Legs

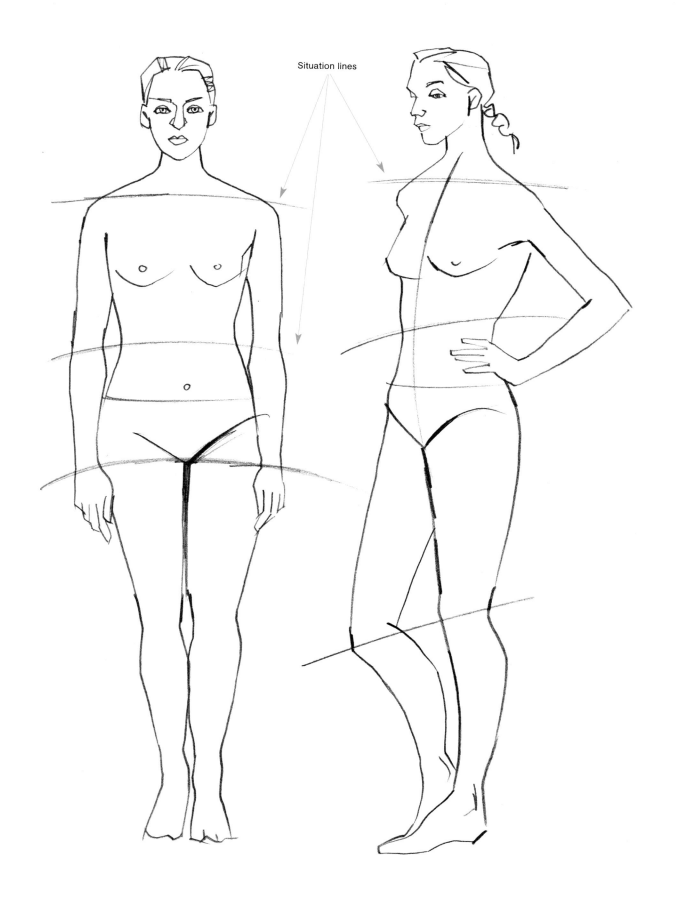

Situation lines

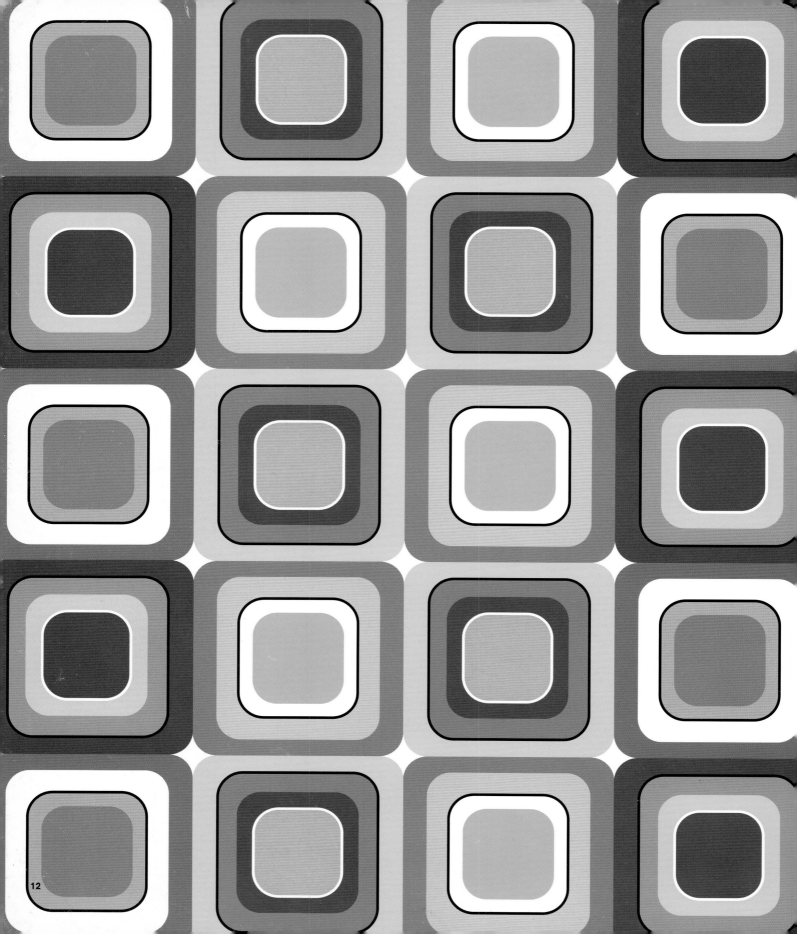

Standing Up

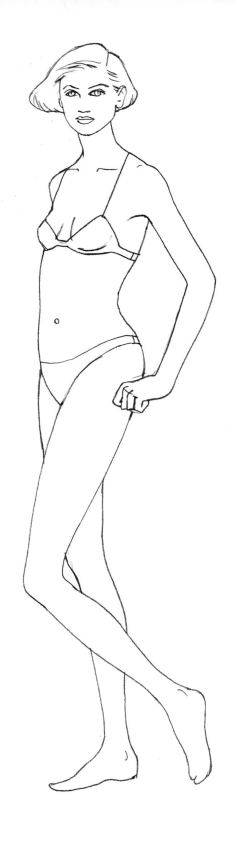

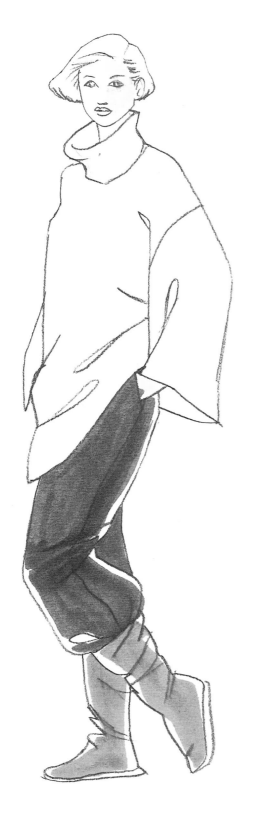

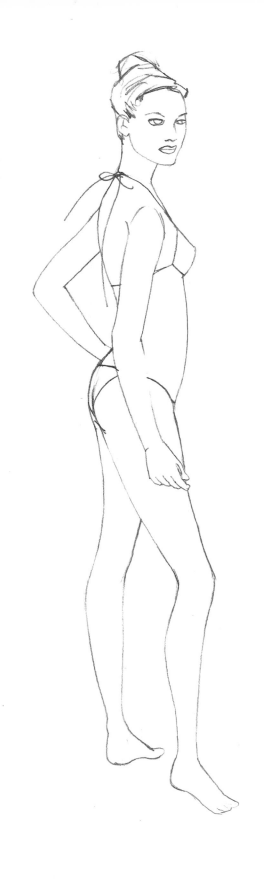
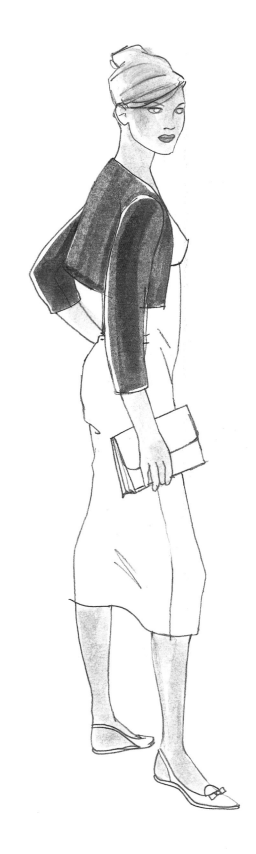

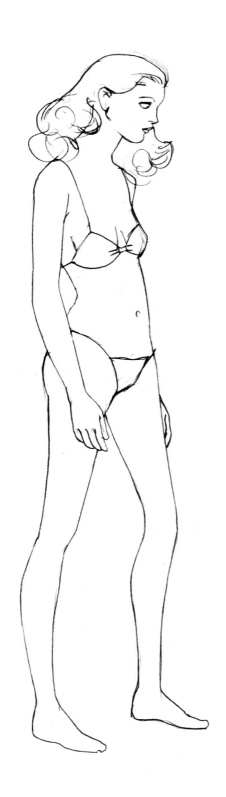

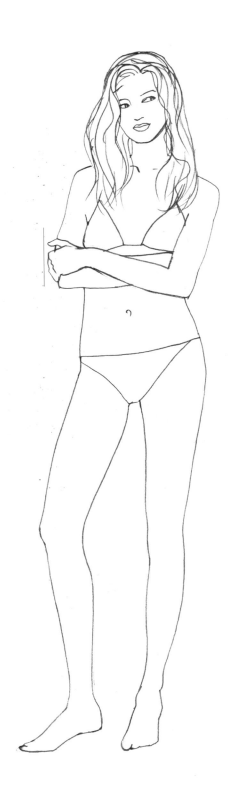

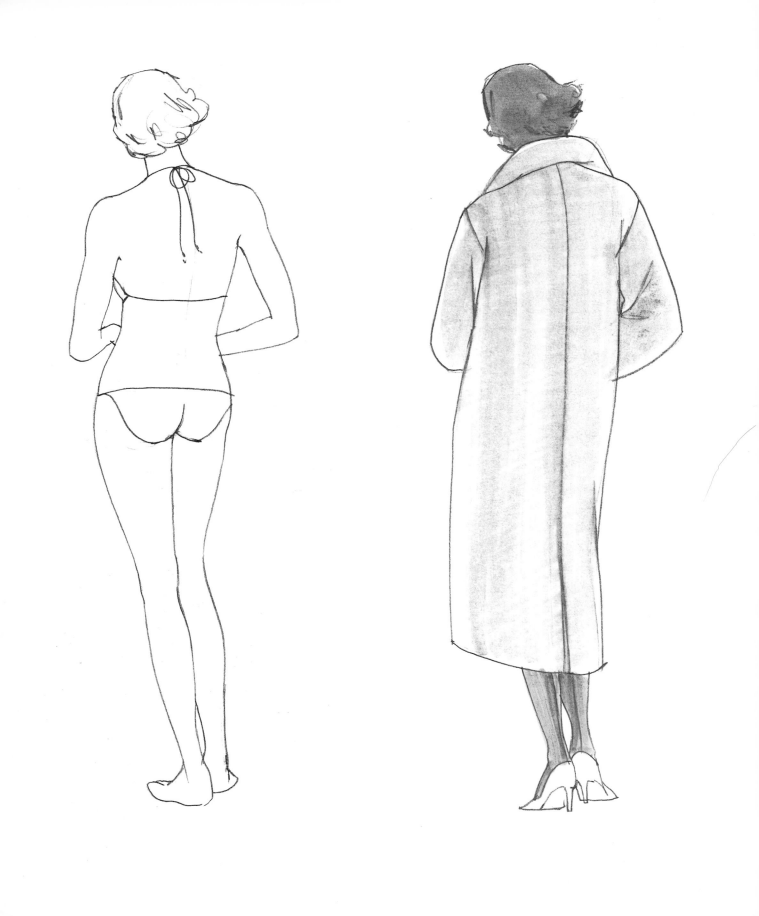

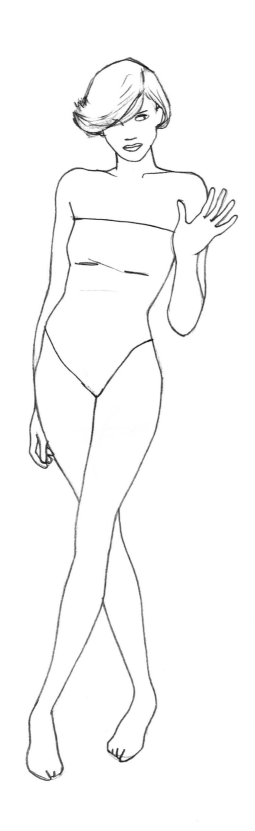
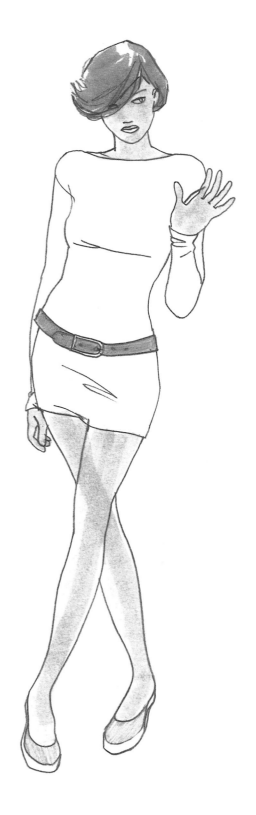

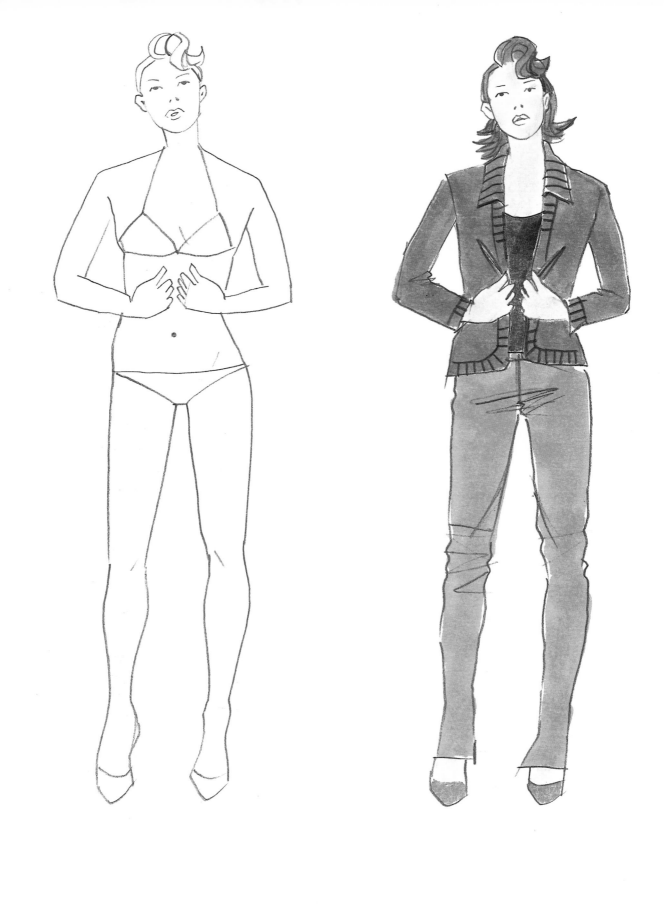

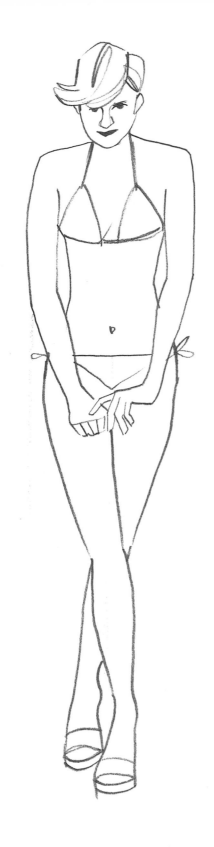

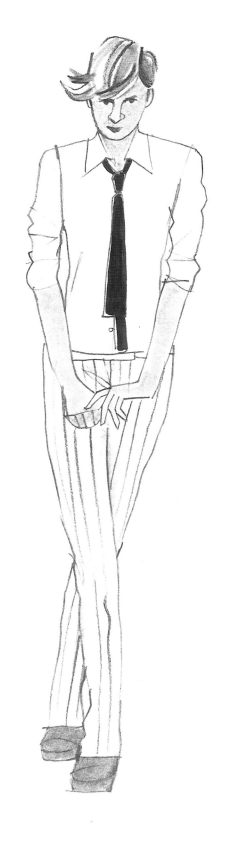

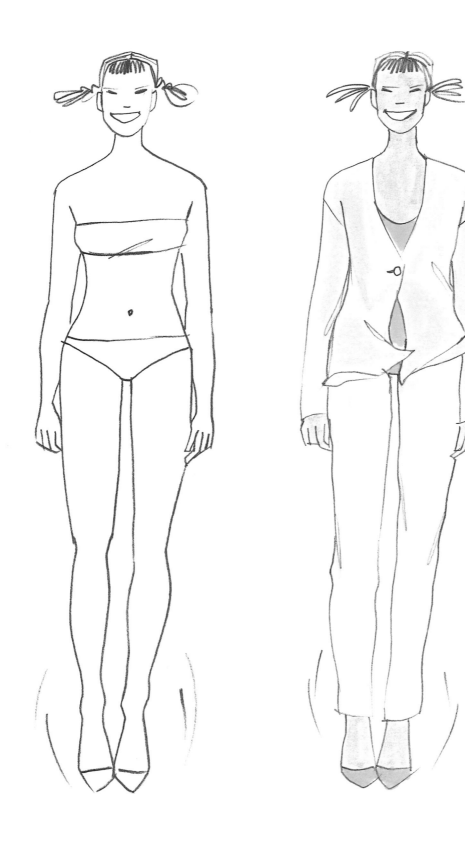

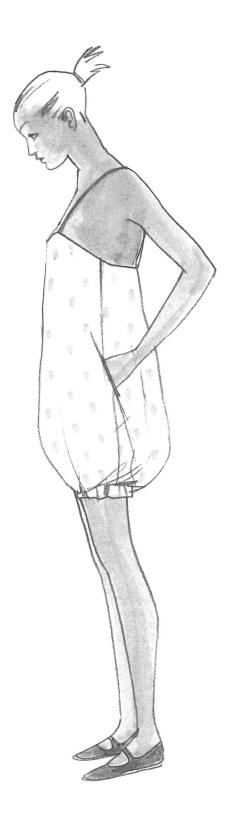

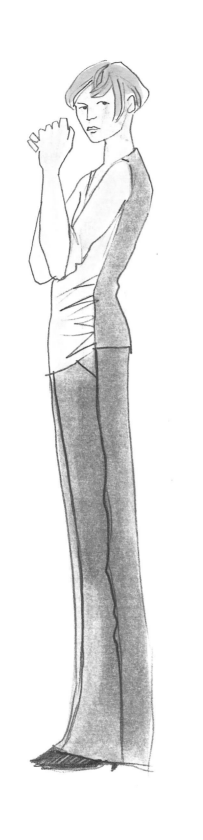
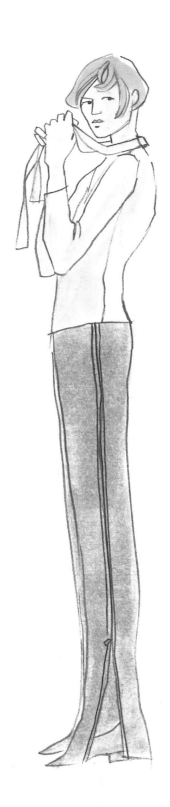

Movements

74

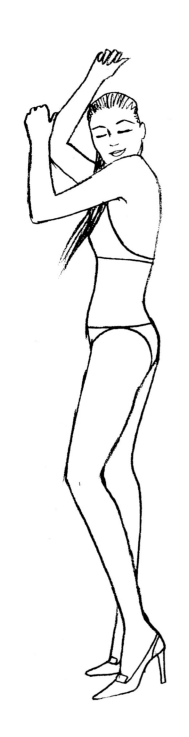
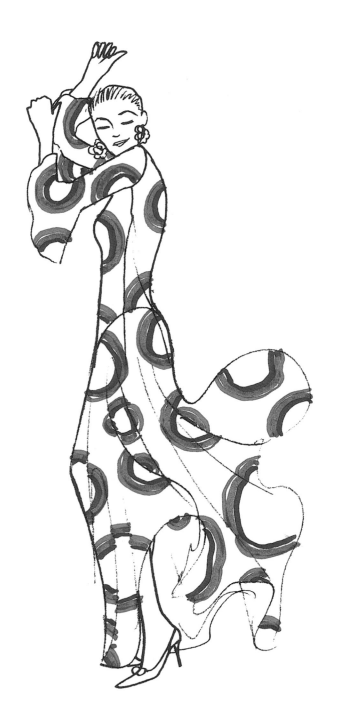

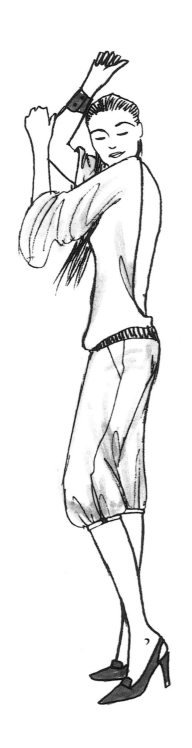

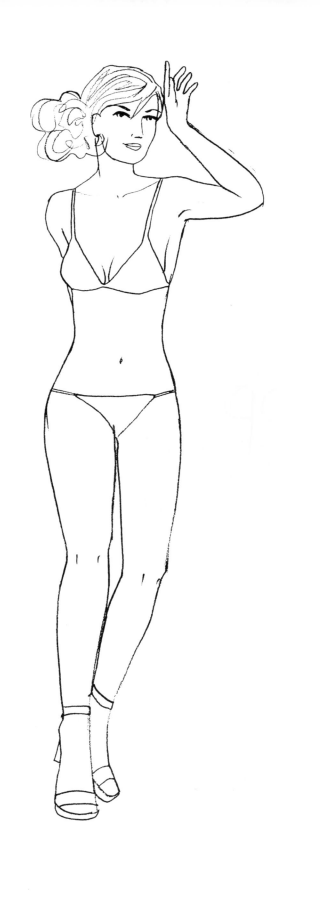
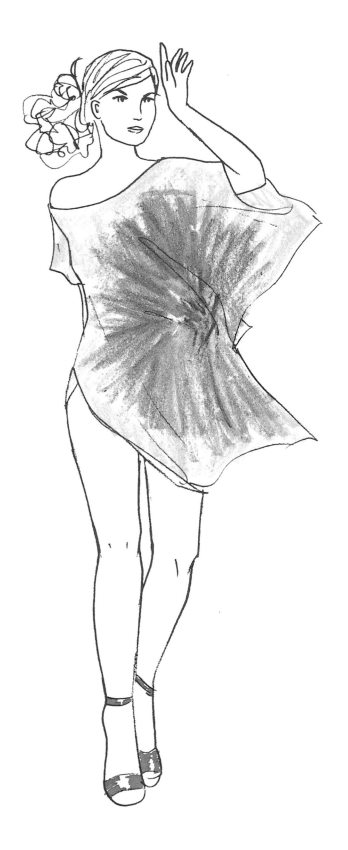

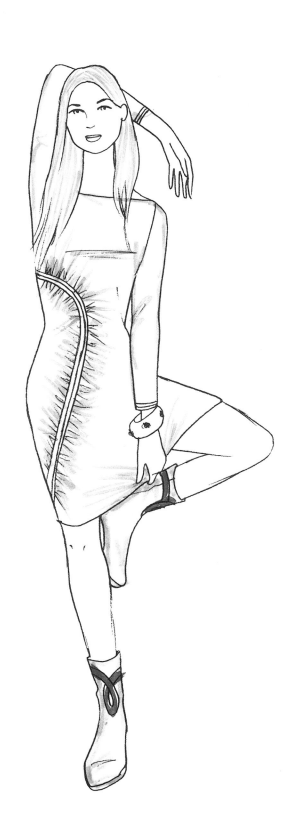

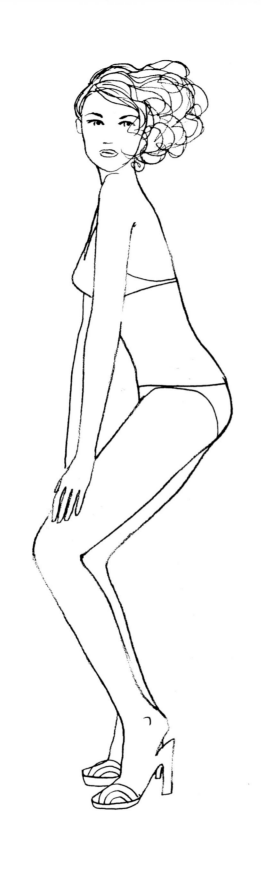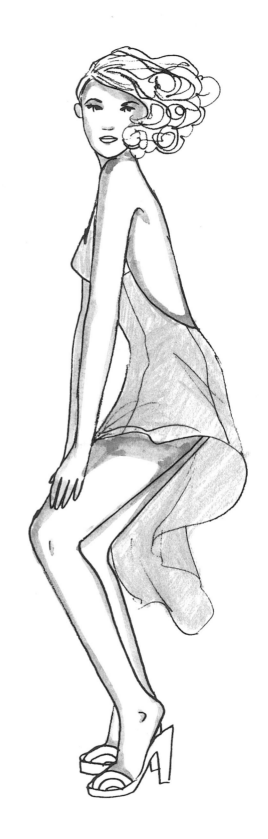

130

Sitting Down

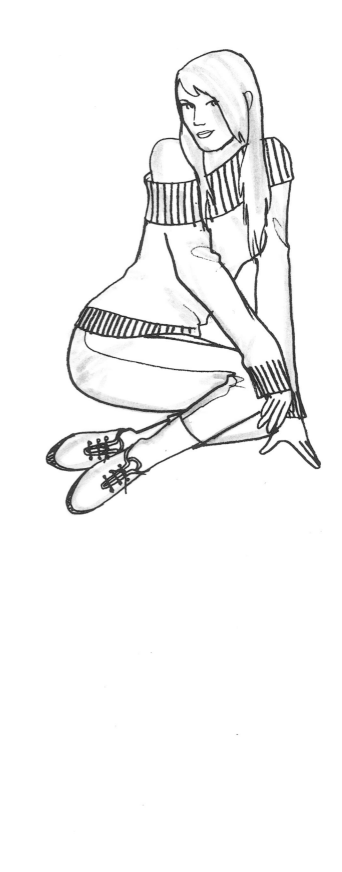

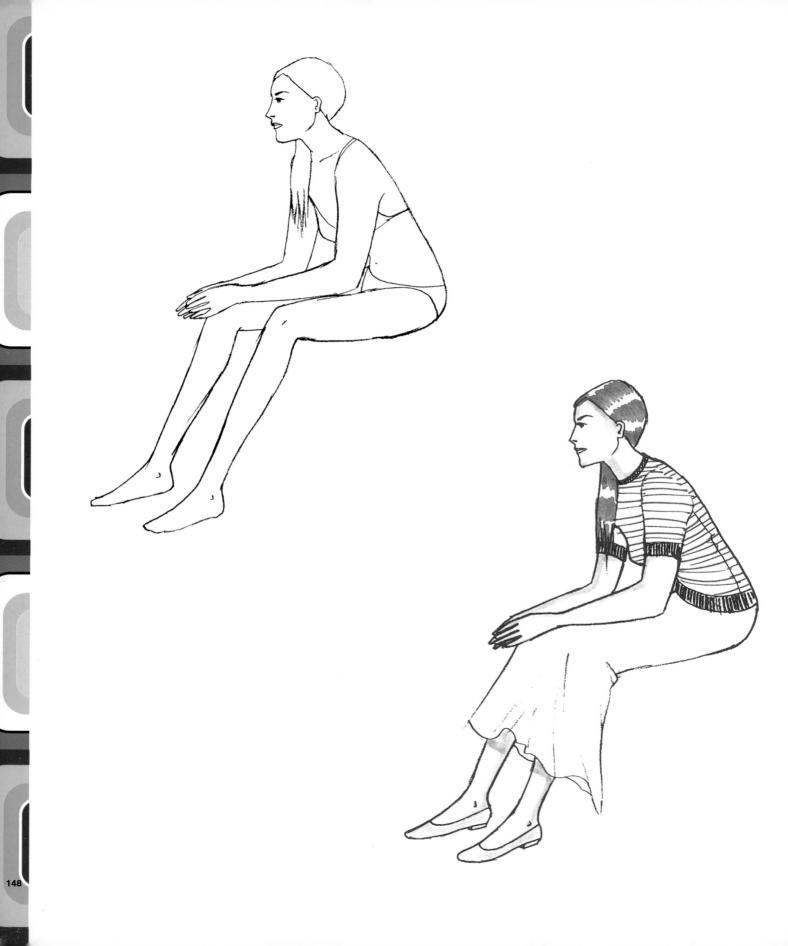

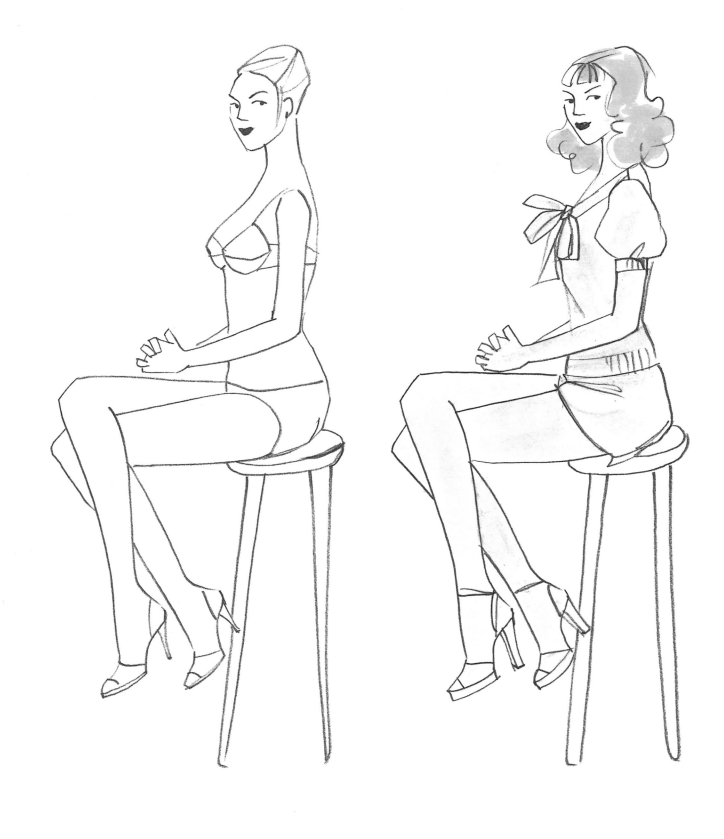

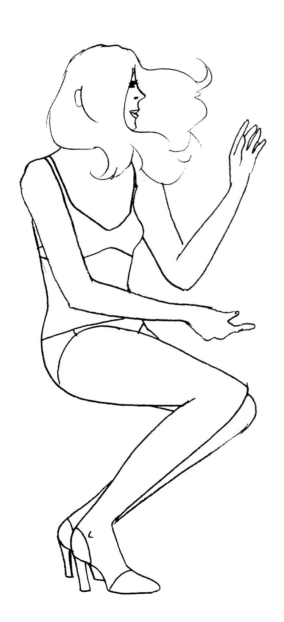

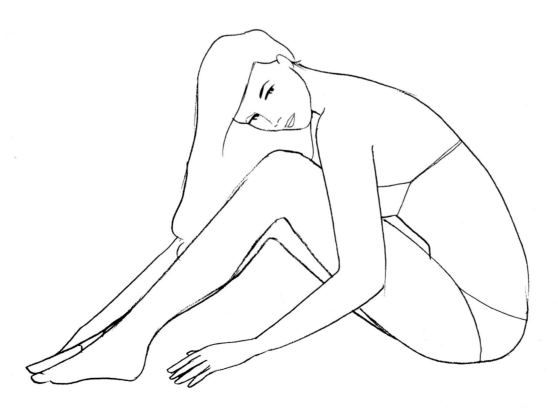

Fashion Schools Directory

North America

United States of America

Academy of Art University
79 New Montgomery Street, 4th floor
San Francisco, CA 94105-3410, USA
P: +1 415 274 2208
www.academyart.edu

American InterContinental University
6600 Peachtree-Dunwoody Road, 500 Embassy Road
Atlanta, GA 30328, USA
www.aiuniv.edu

Bauder College
384 Northyards Boulevard, NW
Suites 190 and 400
Atlanta, GA 30313, USA
P: +1 800 241 3797
www.bauder.edu

Brooks College – Long Beach
4825 E Pacific Coast Highway
Long Beach, CA 90804, USA
P: +1 888 304 9777
www.brookscollege.edu

California Design College
3440 Wilshire Blvd., 10th floor
Los Angeles, CA 90010, USA
P: +1 213 251 3636
www.artinstitutes.edu

FIDM – The Fashion Institute of Design and Merchandising
1010 2nd Avenue
San Diego, CA 92101-4903, USA
P: +1 619 235 2049
www.fidm.com

International Academy of Design and Technology, Chicago
One North State Street, Suite 500
Chicago, IL 60602, USA
www.iadtchicago.edu

Paris Fashion Institute
355 West Fourth St.
Boston, MA 02127, USA
P: +1 617 268 0026
www.parisfashion.org

Parsons. The New School for Design
65 5th Av., ground floor
New York, NY 10003, USA
P: +1 212 229 8989
www.parsons.edu

Pratt Institute
144 West 14th Street,
New York, NY 10011, USA
P: +1 212 647 7775
www.pratt.edu

Westwood College
7350 North Broadway
Denver, CO 80221, USA
awarden@westwood.edu
www.westwoodcollege.com

Europe

Belgium

La Cambre
21 Abbaye de La Cambre
B-1000 Brussels, Belgium
P: +32 2 626 17 80
www.lacambre.be

France

LISAA – L'Institut Supérieur des Arts Appliqués
13 Rue Vauquelin
75005 Paris, France
P: +33 01 47 07 17 07
www.lisaa.com

Studio Berçot
P: +33 01 42 46 15 55
studio.bercot@club-internet.fr
www.studio-bercot.com

ESMOD Berlin
Schlesische St. 29/30
Aufgang I & M
10997 Berlin, Germany
P: +49 30 611 22 14
www.esmod.de

ESMOD München
Fraunhofer St. 23 H
80469 Munich, Germany
P: +49 89 201 45 25
www.esmod.de

Italy

Accademia Italiana
Piazza Pitti 15
50125 Florence, Italy
P: +39 0 552 84616
www.accademiaitaliana.com

A. R. Studio Milan Fashion Campus
Via Broggi 7
20129 Milan, Italy
P: +39 02 268 22730
www.fashioncampus.it

Istituto di Moda Burgo
Piazza San Babila 5
20122 Milan, Italy
P: +39 0278 3753
www.imb.it

Istituto Marangoni
Via Verri 4
20121 Milan, Italy
P: +39 02 763 16680
www.istitutomarangoni.com

Polimoda Institute of Fashion Design and Marketing
Via Pisana 77
I-50143 Florence, Italy
P: +39 0 557 39961
www.polimoda.com

Up to Date Academy
Corso Vittorio Emanuele II 15
20122 Milan, Italy
P: +39 0 276 26791
www.fashionuptodate.com

Spain

ESDI – Escola Superior de Disseny
Av. Marquès de Comillas 79-83
08202 Sabadell, Barcelona, Spain
P: +34 937 274 819
www.esdi.es

United Kingdom

Central Saint Martins College of Art and Design
Catton Street, Holborn
London WC1, United Kingdom
P: +44 (0) 207 514 7027
www.csm.arts.ac.uk

London Centre for Fashion Studies
Bradley Close, White Lion Street
Islington, London N1 9PF, United Kingdom
P: +44 (0) 207 713 1991
www.fashionstudies.com

London College of Fashion
20 John Princes Street
London W1G 0BJ, United Kingdom
P: +44 (0) 207 514 7407
www.fashion.arts.ac.uk

Royal College of Art
Kensingtin Gore
London SW7 2EU, United Kingdom
P: +44 (0) 207 590 4444
www.rca.ac.uk

The Arts Institute at Bournemouth
Wallisdown, Poole
Dorset BH12 5HH, United Kingdom
P: +44 (0) 120 253 3011
www.aib.ac.uk

University College for the Creative Arts
New Dover Road
Canterbury, Kent CT13AN, United Kingdom
P: +44 (0) 122 781 7302
www.ucreative.ac.uk

continued on page 192

Africa & Oceania

South Africa

Elizabeth Galloway Academy of Fashion Design
26 Techno Park
Stellenbosch
7600 Western Cape, South Africa
P: +27 (021) 88 00 77 5
www.safashionacademy.com

Australia

Elizabeth Bence School of Fashion
Level 2, 793-795 Pacific Highway
Gordon NSW 2072, Australia
P: +61 2 9498 7240
www.thefashionschool.com.au

Whitehouse Institute of Design
Level 3, 55 Liverpool Street
Sydney NSW 2000, Australia
P: +61 2 9267 8799
www.whitehouse-design.edu.au

Asia

China

The Hong Kong Polytechnic University
Corea A, 1st. Floor
Hung Hom, Kowloon
Hong Kong, China
P: +852 2766 5454
www.sd.polyu.edu.hk

India

Pearl Academy of Fashion
A 21/13, Naraina Industrial Area, Phase II
New Delhi 110028, India
P: +414 176 93-94
www.pearlacademy.com

Japan

Bunka Fashion College
3-22-1, Yoyogi, Shibuya-ku
151-8522 Tokyo, Japan
P: +81 (0)3 3299 2202
www.bunka-fc.ac.jp